CATHERINE PHIL MacCARTHY grew up in County Limerick. She took an honours degree in English at University College Cork, post-graduate studies in drama at Trinity College Dublin, and at Central School of Speech and Drama, London. She has worked part-time at the Drama Centre, University College Dublin, since 1990, and also gives workshops in creative writing at the Irish Writers' Centre. She was awarded an Arts Council Bursary in 1994, and was Writer in Residence for the City of Dublin in the same year. She is currently the editor of *Poetry Ireland*.

GW00578352

the blue globe

p o e m s

Catherine Phil MacCarthy

THE
BLACKSTAFF
PRESS
BELFAST

First published in 1998 by
The Blackstaff Press Limited
3 Galway Park, Dundonald, Belfast BT16 0AN, Northern Ireland
with the assistance of
The Arts Council of Northern Ireland

Catherine Phil MacCarthy has asserted her right under the
Copyright Designs and Patents Act 1988 to be identified as
the author of this work.

Typeset by Techniset Typesetters, Newton-le-Willows, Merseyside

Printed in Ireland by ColourBooks Limited

A CIP catalogue record for this book
is available from the British Library

ISBN 0-85640-619-8

for
Renate Ahrens-Kramer
and
Ann O'Donoghue

for
Jane Williams

In the depths of the winter
I finally learned that there lay in me
an invincible summer.

ALBERT CAMUS

ACKNOWLEDGEMENTS

Some of these poems have previously appeared in: *Atlanta Review*, *Cimarron Review*, *Compost*, *Crab Orchard Review*, *f/m*, *Home*, *Jumping off Shadows*, *Lifelines 3*, *Literary Review*, *A Part of Ourselves*, *Poetry Ireland Review*, *Responding to Leopardi*, *Sunday Tribune*, UCD *Women's Studies Journal*, and *Writing Women*.

'The barefoot singer' and 'Cowboys and Indians' originally appeared in *College English*.

CONTENTS

III   THE BAREFOOT SINGER

I

THE BLUE GLOBE

THE BLUE GLOBE

You could dig a hole so deep
you'd get to Australia
as clay rich in earthworms
swivelled on the tip
of my garden shovel,

and I pondered how
people could walk
upside down on
the other side of the planet
and not fall off the ground.

The hole I was digging
gave way to a burrow of darkness
all the way down
mile after mile
through the earth.

And the blue globe in school
turned in my hands
on the path from here
to Sydney, shifting
the axis of the known

world spinning between
my fingers with questions
of scale and gravity.
A ripe apple falls
from the Beauty of Bath

in the orchard. My eyes
fathom red earth
at the bottom of a line,
conjure at its very source –
sunshine.

THE MOMENT IT STOPPED

When the phone rang
the blinds were drawn on the sun.
I'm sorry, love, but Joe is dead.

Who's Joe? I said. He waited
for the penny to drop.
I went through Joes in my head.

No one I knew well. Except.
The phone was an asp.
I flung it hard. Down by the sea

three cormorants splayed wings,
stood erect on low rocks.
White breakers blew back

a chiffon scarf, the sky
was cloudless blue, mid-July.
Please, Dad, have a heart.

Don't go yet. Give me
your hatless able-bodied self
saying, 'We might now',

as if you hadn't quite heard,
as if you could for my sake
turn back. Already laid out,

your head wrapped in a bandage,
you looked like a prize calf,
Gulliver held down with string,

the parlour not big enough
for death. Outside wasn't dark
yet. Nothing like the furled

puce heads of roses in our lawn.
I used to pull the petals off,
looking for their hearts,

pollen dust, sometimes a wasp
in my hand. Below the hedge,
your spade on the ground,

I expected chalk to outline
the way you fell, face down,
struggling for breath,

one knee bent like a child's in bed,
arguing with the ground,
your pain scorching the earth.

My fingers trace grass searching
for your wrist, your pulse,
the moment it stopped.

FAMILIAR

That mole under the eye
just the same, your face
all at once furrows and plains,
a felt geography in my hands
breaking open words,
constant, tolerant, friend.

Though my eyes are level
with yours taking me in,
you ask innocently
how long it's been
since you swung me
to the ceiling.

My fingers long
to touch your face warm
and cool at the same time,
find themselves checked
by a deep reserve
and the scent of aftershave.

WITCH

She
squats in the yard,
riddling the ground with a twig

in front of the child
you are,
small enough to see

her long creased thighs,
sun-yellow shift,
cradle

the grassy earth.
In a second she will
rise,

her black hair flying,
dandle earthworms
on the stick,

laugh
and fling them
down your neck.

UNDER MY SKIN

In the school holidays
you wrote to me. Described
the amber and purple of sunset
as if I was there with you.

I grew up in the country.
Never knew what to write back,
as if no words could name loss
or how we told the weather

from our gate by the Galtees.
Blue as the faded ink of the Himalayas
for cutting a meadow, slopes
green and close meant rain.

Seagulls feeding in the old garden,
a storm over the Shannon.
At night the moon was a lantern
in the back yard when my father

went to check the cattle.
Dark nights, he searched under the stairs
for the good lamp, pitched bad cess
to blackness. I pressed

wildflowers to the page I sent you.
Your colours stayed with me.
Those landscapes are
the earth under my skin.

WHEN THERE'S WAR

You saw what happened. The yard deserted
apart from a great white enamel basin full of blood,
left to stand after your mother plunged her hands in
like a Greek heroine to knead bread crumbs,
spice, seasoning. Everyone was somewhere else,
the excitement over and you could hear

the birds again, flitting and calling to each other
from the slate ridge on the roof to the trees
at the back – finches, blackbirds, swallows.
You watched the port-wine surface clog and film
and ran messages with spoils for the neighbours
after tea, in the sunshine across fields.

The screeching echoed in your head.
Some terror in the sound was what you imagined
war to be as you stood with hands over ears
watching the altar of sacrifice. All the better
to see you with, my dear, said the Big Bad Wolf
to Little Red Riding Hood, in the happy-ever-after

world you had trouble even then
believing, ears unable to hear themselves any more,
all the better to eat you, as the throat is slit.
You can still see the small girl behold for the first time
how life goes on despite everything, air cool
on bare skin, her body easing into a yawn.

You walk in from the grass one evening
and though the world as you know it is cured in salt,
there is that first thing, smell, call it what you will,
spring, only a matter of time, the earth's urge
to blossom. Young tendrils in a steady move
towards fruition.

SPELLS

Smocked bathing suits
rolled in towels

were passports to the car.
Go, if you're going!

All reproach, my mother
shook holy water

from the glass font
of the Child of Prague.

It wet my skin like rain
and evaporated,

with my father
at the wheel singing

to a scorcher of a day
that shrunk currents,

drowning waves,
the tide itself

to wrack pools
of anemone and sea moss,

a waterline at sunset
ebbing at my ankles

and traces
coming home

under my clothes
of Atlantic salt.

HELEN

In slim rib tights,
not thick and woolly
from wear
like mine,

hair not short
and tied on a leash
but woven down her back
in a plait,

books neither
dog-eared nor
missing but open
and crisp on the desk,

no blobs
or thumbprints,
a gold nib
lightly dipped,

tongue neither
swallowed nor lost,
the right answer,
by heart.

CHARMS

Thistles. Nettles.
In the long grass,
a hot afternoon.

The calves of my legs
stung. Dock leaves
rubbed to juice

trickled green
on the burn.
What time was it then?

I reached for
dandelion clocks.
Whispered your name.

Whole moons frayed
under my breath.
One o'clock, two,

loves me, loves me
not. The answer?
A bald stem.

CUBA 1962

We were down in the barn
washing the milking machine.
I stood in dusk looking out
at swallows dipping across the yard
and over the hedge, tails sharp as scissors.

The far side, a wall of roses basked,
without seeing I could tell,
light and dark pink from
times I looked into their heads
and breathed the scent.

My mother was crying. There was
nothing but noise from the machine.
All I knew was she couldn't tell me
why. Her tears fell clean into water,
a stór agus a stóirín,

coming from deep down in the chest,
for saying goodbye
to passage ships, a crowd
gathered at the water's edge
as if it was the last day on earth.

It made me think of the three
black days we were promised
when the world would end.
No one allowed out, not even
to milk the cows. A leaflet from

the government said big words
I could only spell, windows
and doors hid with sacks of grain,
for when things happened to the air,
little grey dots going red all over.

GREEK

Old books in my room
under hats
on top of the wardrobe

brown hardcovers
I tipped on the floor
opened,

never having known
Patrick,
home from school

at sixteen with pneumonia
he caught in the rain
after rugby.

In my hands a dust-covered
book with no pictures,
his quill signature,

still-to-be-cut leaves
of a favourite grammar
describing him in symbols

that stopped at gamma.

ACTS OF GOD

When thunder crashed on the roof
like heavy furniture

I felt the way blind
downstairs in the dark,

found everyone
round the kitchen table

counting seconds.
Lightning lit the tap,

cracked the floor like a whip,
made me jump out of my skin.

The unconcerned outline
of my father's shoulders,

my mother somewhere
foraging for matches,

the pitch of my sisters'
voices, the baby upstairs

sleeping – small things
that hold us.

Then in the hush,
a downpour.

SPRING CLEANING

On the top shelf
a wire of household bills
keeled like a spinning top,

your missal fat as a tick
with mortuary cards and prayers,
a Cadbury's box of letters

you read fragments from,
knitting patterns (Grace Kelly
blondes, FOR MEN in cable sweaters).

Everything from used stamps
saved for the missions
to clippings from the paper

spilled across the table,
recipes for boiled fruitcake,
blancmange, and how to keep

a soufflé from dropping in the oven.
In the end I uncovered something
by accident. My face blushed

at what it meant. Clipping
after clipping of old newsprint
on coping with depression.

NEW YEAR'S EVE

My sisters were gone to a dance.
I could hear church bells tolling
three miles away. It carried me
to my knees in the dark,

unhinging the window latch
to open out the casement
on frost glistening in moonlight,
satin along a slate roof,

the rustle of a cow asleep,
my body naked in the rush of cold
under night things, my head
turned by nothing except stars.

AT SEVENTEEN

For months before at night upstairs
places all across the States you wanted to see
spilled from your mouth – Salt Lake,
Grand Canyon, the Falls at Niagara –

in bed, the map spread across our knees,
your first real summer holiday,
both of us trying to separate memory
from hearsay, locate an emigrant tree,

letters from Aunt Kate in Chicago
we only ever saw in a graduation photo,
the doll she sent when you were five
and I was too young to recall, standing again

on the table no less a wonder than
the unholy sights you were destined to see –
Liberty, Ellis Island, Disney – me ready
to follow you all the way to the frontier

and across the Rockies at Butte, Montana,
to the beach at Malibu,
then on to the Mojave Desert before I fell asleep,
we'll see, my head full of the Atlantic

crossing, a passageway for generations,
long before you boarded a 747 at Shannon
and a Greyhound bus that wove a trail
much farther than the relatives you went to see,

and I was more than willing to believe it was me
standing on the crest of a waterfall
as the heavens opened and steam rose,
a deluge of torrents thundering down

hundreds of feet, my hair a halo of spray,
my face wet from no tears,
my head light from the rock bottom sound,
feet happy enough to fly

for the sheer hell of wanting to know what it's like
to pour down a virtual ocean
now that I've made the break
there's no holding me.

And who wouldn't want to believe I was far away
from the crush of slow dances,
my back a hall of streaming condensation,
a wallflower in the sway

of beer and left feet,
a summer of solitary walks to the road
in close thundery heat,
and staying up late to read

with Tom Jones and 'The green green grass
of home' at close-down on TV,
the night long before I toss off the quilt
in the too warm double bed

and my thumb slides under the pillow
to the transistor dial at my ear
and the room fills
with the voice of Janis Ian.

AWAKENINGS

You keep coming to mind –
opening a blouse
to slip off a bra,
your breast in my hand

pale and round,
faded coral around the nipple,
like my sister glimpsed
inside a cotton nightdress

at sixteen, bathed, scented
and ready for bed.
I hushed from shyness
and wondered if she knew

how beautiful she was.
I was going to be twelve
and slept on the inside
near the wall, her body

my shield against the dark.
When we talked I listened
and lay awake reading
patterns on the wallpaper,

lantern shapes, green
and gold embossed on cream.
Now in that room
where you hold me, my heart

heals. This is how I picture us
when you're gone,
my head on your breast,
your blouse undone.

FABLE

In the story
you heard as a child
they said he threw her
overboard one night

when the Shannon
was at full tide.
So determined was she
not to let go

that it took
all his power
to prise each finger
from the rim of the boat

free. This is how
you see her now,
not the young bride
echoing marriage vows

soon bearing his child,
but fighting the black
swirling river
with every last ounce

of force, her hands frozen
to the stern, knuckles grown
white, white, white.
And when you asked

how this young man could
hear his own woman cry
and fail to turn human
they said nobody knew

what happened that night,
he was out of his mind,
and anyhow he never meant
to make her his wife.

By then you'd seen the house,
the river at eleven miles wide,
the court where
he paid the price.

PRE-RAPHAELITE

You loved the veined fragility
of her wrist, hair in a sheaf to the waist,
the slender hand warming yours
in the pocket of her gaberdine.

You were friends then, strolling
after tea to the Shrine of the Virgin
past the rose garden, the old nun
weeding, a greenhouse of ripe tomatoes.

To impress her you talked of despair,
a window ledge on the fourth floor,
how her voice reined you in
when you woke from a nightmare.

You tested your eyes for glasses,
learned to name-drop French existentialists.
When the nuns raided Holy Angels
they found Sartre's *Nausea*

under your pillow. She had been to
La Rochelle that summer, hummed
'Love the one you're with'
opening her boyfriend's letters.

COWBOYS AND INDIANS

I wanted to sit in your place,
drive beside him
to the dance. Eighteen,
carefully made-up,

raven hair and a scooped
neck. I was just
the gooseberry in the back seat
he'd hardly glanced at

since he was thirteen,
the kid he chased one afternoon
over holes in the sand.
I laughed and ran,

then fell in a pool
bruising my knee, and he
fell on top of me.
Cowboys and Indians at the beach?

No roofs of sheds or apple trees.
My head was in the sea.
When his weight disappeared
the beach was full

of sunshine and tears,
identical striped windbreakers.
Was that why I wanted to
sit beside him

when I turned fourteen,
wishing it was me
he gazed at
in the light of the windscreen

all manners and Brylcreem,
both struggling to make
adult conversation
as we drove together in the dark?

DIVINER

A cleft in the ash halfway up
its beautiful etched bark,
two branches fork

so evenly it could be
a person upside down,
limbs thrust into the blue

spreading a leafy canopy
over me. I used to reach
my hand inside the split

where it curved and knit
to divine something secret,
a lovers' tryst,

words penned on scraps,
at my fingertips, dreams
I never expected to have.

II

SAND GODDESS

WONDERLAND

You are the smooth rock
in whose warm hollow I bask,
like tiny Alice.

LUCY'S SONG

*for Lucy Partington, murdered in 1973,
aged twenty-one years*

Uncover my bones, long dead and clean,
The moon of my skull that gleams in the mire,
Hold me to your breast, carry me unseen

From this vile place, where I have been
Dismembered for years, a brutal lair,
Uncover my bones, long dead and clean.

Blood of my blood, this is no time to keen,
Work by the colour of the dawn air,
Hold me to your breast, carry me unseen.

From the mouth of hell, unthread my spine,
Rib cage, pelvis, sacrum, in order,
Uncover my bones, long dead and clean.

From a chest of oak, let goodness shine,
A jar of honey, music of a choir,
Hold me to your breast, carry me unseen.

Sister, my sister, your love is mine,
I move with you, the silence is clear,
Uncover my bones, long dead and clean,
Hold me to your breast, carry me unseen.

ANCIENT DELTA

Sometimes I follow the tide
out across the strand,

wade at each turn
a stream that trails light

like a coil of fallen hair.
Out there could be

the heart of an ancient delta,
the far bank always

smooth, promising a collar
of white surf on the horizon.

Where I walk is wrinkled
sea floor at the brink of river.

From then on I hear sand,
the call of a curlew,

one ear full of the sea,
the other, muted city.

On the ebbed tide wild geese
flock in the shallows.

I am caught in that stillness
as the light goes,

measuring distances,
not knowing the time,

the way home,
listening for the tide's turn.

BABY

She goes to ground
on the pillow of your breast,
stray hair, buttons,
her closed fist,
a small animal
burrowing earth,
lost to primroses, time,
everything but rest.

SAND GODDESS

On the beach at Smerwick
a figure scooped out of sand —
breast, navel, genitals,
decorated with spirals of shells,
that stove light like
breakers on the shore.

Eyes, nose, mouth, stones.
Seaweed green hair.
There for the spoiling as if
she were the same
as any other castle.
What man and woman divined

a goddess from their play
leaving soundless joy
in the air about her?
Has she no name? Could it be
Duibhne of the black hair
come to restore us to history?

Children take turns lying
in the valley of her thighs
as if birthed from her womb,
and ferried all at once
in the boat of her knees,
they row the stream over stones,

jump out to snuggle at her side,
ask if it's possible to get inside her,
failing that, gingerly lift
the shell of her nipple,
take an eye out of her head
leaving her matter-of-factly blind,

their touching at first
awed by the reality
that a woman is a body
they have never been this close to,
and finally that a woman is a body
even they can dismantle.

MAROONED

The Seine burst its banks. You stayed
in the basement perfecting a clay model.

The river flowed in the door. After dark
levels rose on the wall to the table of

your workbench and all night you sat
above the flood mesmerised by patterns of light

cast by an angry God through branches
on the windowpane. By dawn you were

waiting for the waters to abate across the room,
a beleaguered Noah impatient for signs.

Running water sang in your ears,
the flooded gulleys of a mountainside.

For comfort you stroked the marble head
of a girl who used to live next door.

MIDSUMMER

When she stands out in the grass
holding him in her arms in the last light
at three, or five, or seven years,
his long sleek legs straddling her hips,
hot face buried in her neck,
feeling the day's heat before dark,
how long does it take
for his arms around her neck
to ease their clasp, his full weight
sink onto her chest,
both drugged by night-scented stock,
a pair of late swifts, and both
sure by now it's just to tell
who after all is holding who.

BLASKET SOUND

A hundred yards out from
the island the Atlantic boils
round us in black swells.
The boatman predicts rain,
fishes in the hold for jackets,
leans over to hand them, one
by one. Smells drunk. Our boat
drifts. The prow dips so low
the sea flakes across the faces
of my children. With wet hands
I pull belts tight, struggle at
their waists with zips and clasps.
Tourists lurch on their seats.
The pier we embarked from is
lost in rocks along the coast
where the island rises green.

NATURE STUDY

It might have been you,
the woman with a small boy
bending over a pool below the trees.
Something about the hair,
the gait and silent attention.
Where the ground became
marsh, the water clotted
and filmed, gave way to
rushes and peat sods.

My son went to join in,
curious to see tadpoles
cupped in her open palm
like great black sperm,
watched as she showed him
how to lay his open hand
on the fizzy bottom
and wait for the water
to settle in perfect stillness.

INFESTATION

The gauze cocoon you found
in the ditch, high up attached
like a tent between shoots of briars,
a white dome alive with
centipedes crawling all over it,
down the veins of the bush,
furry brown bodies wriggle
everywhere to feed on leaves.

Inside the silk webs of the tent
are tiny black eggs. I scan
the dense growth of the hedge.
Wild parsley froths at my waist,
grasses, whitethorn, vetch,
a briar rose, all flourish.
Suddenly nothing is safe.

EARTHMOVER

Do they pull the old one down
and a crane lifts in the new?
my seven-year-old asked of the moon.

In his tree house all summer
building with nails and hammer,
dreams of earthmovers

and diggers, that even mysteries
of the universe, light and darkness,
flow from pipes and cables.

THE SHOW

A giant turd the hippo
steams on the earth. The keeper
enters her patch, sets down
a feeding bucket. Her eyes
stay closed. Onlookers wait.
He strokes the massive face,
sidles round her impassive
head, rests a hip against
her neck, leans over to
slap her cheek once.
Her eyes blink
closed but the huge jaw
drops ivory fangs
and the world is
the coral pink inside
of her mouth, yawning
tongue and palate –
the minute we see it
we are falling
down her throat.

HELIUM

Like when Rachel let go the balloon
getting out of the car,
and before we knew where we were
its string toyed beyond our hands,

your words untethered my heart,
tinsel pink and weightless,
high as the slate roof and soaring
over our house, good as lost in the breeze

that buoys it, way into the blue
beyond the garden wall,
from where we gaze in wonder at its path,
a gaudy speck too small to see

against the pink and white
of chimney stacks marking the coast,
about to cross a line,
from where there is no return.

VESUVIUS

In the woods
round Lake Albano
were violets more fragrant
than at home, and white

ones I'd never seen
anywhere. The hill town
each dawn was the same
fiery crescent

glimpsed from a window
in the shower.
My path went down below
the chapel with

Bellini frescos,
mother and infant
above the great door,
past the terrace wall

into a silence of fallen leaves,
a sharp downturn
over water I'd yet to explore
said by locals to be

icy even in summer,
my body resisting the steep
descent to the core,
jet-black, volcanic.

WHAT ON EARTH?

The books you sent back with
a card saying barely a word
about yourself left me puzzled,

turning it over in my hand
to wonder if something happened
since I saw you last,

and what on earth an upside-down
bunch of orange and crimson dahlias
tied to dry on an off-white peeling wall

above a hyacinth bulb in a glass vase,
the web of roots growing in clear water,
stands for. And what

is the cause and meaning anyway
of such relics, are you telling me –
death and preservation?

WITNESS

Beside me her face was stained
by tears she kept rubbing away
with her hands, like a defenceless child.

Inside the house they renovated
together, her things were packed
and labelled in one corner.

I carried suitcases one by one
down the hall to the door
feeling gradually an accomplice.

When she was ready to go
there was one thing left to show me –
the darkroom, a bare laboratory

with scraps of film and exposures.
For minutes we talked over
a tray of solution, connecting words

like *brightness* and *timing*,
my eye beginning to focus
on the close-up of a couple,

her hands a gesture of how
the image clarifies, then darkens,
at the moment of definition.

ENDLESS SONG

You asked so often
how I would like it to be,

your face a silent request
as if it mattered how I felt

and my will could be a gift
in the final reckoning of things.

I bent my head, tendered
love, wanting to see us

always as we were, cradling
an invisible bond

and ready to tune in
to where all wishes end

and begin in an endless song.
I thought you could stop time

and the season we turned to
would always be spring –

our separate lives over years
a fluent blossom.

I thought you could ease pain
– exorcise the thorn –

my wish was an open palm
and I was wrong.

MIRROR

That first day I saw you
as a widow you wore carmine,
your skin next to it a translucent
membrane. You sat inert
in the chair as a waiting child.
On your lap the right hand
held your wrist. You'd forgotten
your watch and asked for the time –
it was just noon. I looked at
your eyes, the delicate veins
around temple and brow
visible as a newborn child's,
and you gazed back at me from
under those lids, your whole head
exposed and fragile as a baby's
after the trauma of birth.

HARVEST

Under the picnic table
on the grass, lavender flowers –
the children picked to sell

for pennies to passers-by
at the end of our road –
strewn. As if Persephone herself

fled. I gathered them up
stem by stem, each one an offering
to allay a panic of my own,

and placed the small sheaf
where it would keep and dry,
colours deepening as the weeks

passed, ready for when I would
give it to you in shades of smoky blue
fragrance burning in my hand.

RECORD

Afraid of losing you I've taken to
reading about fossils to see what
lasts. It only makes it worse. How
spines and ribs of skeleton fish

once embedded in sea mud turn
over millions of years to stone,
more faithful than a lover's heart
sworn on the bark of a tree. How pristine

an image this kauri leaf's fate is when
pressed into limestone. How long have we?
Why struggle with words to celebrate
this love sprung over time from

the earth's crust? Instead I'll turn
to moss and fern in timeless stone.

III

THE BAREFOOT SINGER

THE BAREFOOT SINGER

When I found it broken
on the mantelpiece I looked

to find what, ages ago,
you brought me from Greece.

A terracotta plate
with a barefoot singer

clad in loose robes,
seated on a rock

inside a frieze,
plucking the strings of a lyre.

Around her tall grasses lean,
and on a crag a cormorant.

You might say that
time took it to pieces,

left the clay brittle
and me in silence

matching fragments
of her parted lips

to piece the story
of all that comes between us.

CONQUEST

When the day finally came
you never said goodbye.
He boarded the *Terra Nova*
and the Antarctic was
worse than another woman,

volatile and puritan,
drawing him into
the Southern Ocean.
You knew in the end
he would die to claim it,

distances, blizzards,
frozen temperatures.
After the baby was born
he began to sleep
in the spare room.

Late one night
in the month before going
you heard him
charting his territory,
the way he later

entered the Circle,
a slow rasp of metal
then thunder – glaciers
of blue ice, a huge melt,
the blood and violet of December seas.

CREPE

You were wearing that dress.
Crepe. His eyes scarcely dared
to look. Dove grey with a print
of indigo. It unveiled the delicate
line of your collarbone,
breast, hips. Your eyes,
downcast sultry, looked to
right and left, brows a thin
crescent, lips cherry red,
hair dark silk. You seemed to say
touch, waiting there barefoot.
How he wanted you then
to turn and lead him back to
the small room on the third floor,
where he would touch
his lips to yours for the first time,
cup his hand over your breast
and feel your heart wild
under his palm as a small bird.

THIRST

Land soaks water
in a parched basin
of scrub and trees,
underwater green

and empty for miles
of plain – like the dried-up
bed of an inland sea
my body memorises

your movement over me
in a tide of light and air
so briny, so clear,
it's shimmering.

DEEP INSIDE

When you entered me the first time
you rose deep inside.
I looked past dusk in the window
at the ascending bark

of the ash tree and aftergrass
in the field sloping away
to the ditch. Miles down,
the valley lightened

to meadow green and corn
where the Barrow at a turn
wound to a glint. To hold still
my eyes followed water

I couldn't see,
shaded under the bridge
into sunshine past reeds.
Soon we reached the sheer slide

where three rivers meet
the rocking waters of an estuary
and the tide comes and goes
in a fast channel to the open sea.

FIRES

My anger was red as the fire we lit
at nightfall in a bed of stones
gathered by the lake shore,
along with dry sticks and turf

black as pitch, your ringed hand
reaching down to bank sod after sod
in a neat cairn, a fire god
from the time of Fionn

in the shade of whitethorn,
cooking supper. I watched you
bask in the glow of heat, seeing it turn
to liquid flame, stir and fuel

its burning heart in readiness for the feast,
and heedless of its force as one
who sucked pain from his thumb
after touching the blistered salmon.

LOGAN

When the plane rose into the night
trailing from its great wing
Nantucket, the Cape, and farther in
a massive web of light,
the pilot prompted us to look left
and find the moon in eclipse,
charting our route north and east
along the coast of Maine.

I wondered where you were
and gazed through the porthole
at a star in darkness
and the earth a shadow penny
stuck motionless on the moon's face,
and you down there unknown
to me and vanished in a constellation,
Boston at the edge of water.

MIGRATION

Getting out of the car in blanched gloom,
we stood stiff after the long drive,
me checking for stars, a cusp of moon
(it could be another planet),
you talking about fishing cabins
lit with small lanterns over holes
in the ice all through February,
already packed away for next winter.
The frozen tennis ball you picked
from the ground and tossed in my hand,
I caught and returned out of instinct,
its cold sphere reminding me I'd landed
a continent away from springtime.

DARK POOLS

You weren't Narcissus
when you offered a chair, a drink,
and the dark pools of your eyes,
wanting to hear me out
with talk of skin and bone
but words no longer came

and your eyes were everything.
I was Echo in the woods
filled with longing
and condemned to lose my tongue,
never able to speak first,
only repeat your words,

here, *here* and *come*,
when I saw you in passing.
Since your eyes scorned me
you've been cursed
and gaze in a clear spring
consumed in your own reflection.

WINDFALLS

At sunrise we started
the long drive home from
the valley of the Dordogne.
Over the brow of a hill,
the river behind us,
the car swerved past plums
there for the taking
– a whole summer red and golden,
as if each tree,
weary of being laden
in such temperatures,
overnight lifted her branches
to shed the crop. For no one.
To begin over a new season.
The road was empty.
There were too many
to gather, some so ripe
they split open, juice
and flesh on dusty gravel.

FACING THE MUSIC

You ran through the house
in bare feet and shorts
like a wounded animal,

the bathroom door
banging behind you,
closing on sobs,

deep and rhythmical
as ancient music in a Moorish city.
Notes that tickled

the skin of your spine
where you once played on a balcony,
and hauled you down

a white-walled street
pungent with herbs and sweet almond,
to an open door,

Muslim women inside
keening on a mosaic floor,
his body.

GLACIAL

A deep sorrow, the lake
we came across at evening
after walking all day,
our path rose above
tree line on Mount Washington.

Water opened out
under a towering ridge
clear to the bottom
and strangely green
in that air of revelation,

untouched since the ice age
and far from anything human.

ANTIGONE

What kind of fury made you
steal out at dawn
and again at noon

hardly seeing
where you were going,
your head down,

to seek out his body
left past the city
for carrion?

When you found it
exposed to the skies
you laid it out

with bare hands
like the child who played
in the sand at

burying her brother,
as he shut his laughing eyes
tight to wait

motionless,
while the fine dust falls
on the honey brown skin

of his legs,
pale valley of his neck
on ribs of divine hair.

THE PILGRIM'S WAY

One morning I rambled the Green
      Road above Kilmalkedar
          going

back centuries in the silence
      and heat. Past a sundial
          in stone

in the graveyard, ogham writing,
      a passage rose, closing with
          fuchsia.

My whole year wound to a murmur
      of wild bees, underground streams,
          beyond

the tears to a shoal of dolphins
      out in the bay making for
          the sea.